# CALLEDTOSHEPHERD

# CALLEDTOSHEPHERD

## 52 WEEKLY DEVOTIONS FOR PASTORS AND MINISTRY LEADERS

### WRITTEN BY JOHN CROSBY

## AMBASSADOR INTERNATIONAL
GREENVILLE, SOUTH CAROLINA & BELFAST, NORTHERN IRELAND

www.ambassador-international.com

# Called to Shepherd
## 52 Weekly Devotions for
## Pastors and Ministry Leaders

Printed in the United States of America

Hardcover ISBN: 978-1-62020-023-0
Paperback ISBN: 978-1-64960-265-7
eISBN: 978-1-62020-039-1

Cover Design by Matthew Mulder
Page Layout by Kelley Moore of Points & Picas

AMBASSADOR INTERNATIONAL
Emerald House
427 Wade Hampton Blvd.
Greenville, SC 29609, USA
www.ambassador-international.com

AMBASSADOR BOOKS
The Mount
2 Woodstock Link
Belfast, BT6 8DD, Northern Ireland, UK
www.ambassador-international.com

*The colophon is a trademark of Ambassador*

*Called to Shepherd* is dedicated to the countless
pastors and ministry leaders who have reached
out to me since childhood, inspiring and shaping my life
through teaching, preaching, counseling, serving,
accountability, and friendship. It is also dedicated to
thousands of men and women serving in the trenches of
day-to-day ministry, overcoming the temptations of pride
and fear while faithfully seeking to love and honor our
God and the people they have been trusted to serve.

Thank you.

John Crosby has been blessed with the gift of clarity. These devotions are clear, challenging and helpful to young and old pastors and ministry leaders alike. Every week's devotion speaks to issues that simply must be addressed in the lives of those who are called to shepherd.

Portable, practical and palatable; this helpful resource is a green pasture for both sheep and shepherds.

**Kenny Grant**, Kenny Grant Evangelistic Ministries

Any Christian who has ever led in any way—as a pastor, teacher, administrator, ministry team leader—is sensitive to the challenges of leading as Christ would lead. They have dealt with subtle and not-so-subtle temptations to abdicate to a power, do-it-my-way style of leading. John Crosby demonstrates the need, qualities, and attitudes of those who would lead well, for the right reasons, and to the right end. I've found his pithy, penetrating devotions a blessing to my soul.

**Eleanor A. Daniel**, Dorothy Keister Walker Professor
of Christian Education Emeritus, Emmanuel
School of Religion, Johnson City, TN

I have found John's short devotions to be loaded with wisdom. Each weekly writing gives a key thought to remember and take with you throughout the week. A great way for busy ministry leaders to start each week.

**Dicky Clark**, Vice President of Field Ministry, Southeast Coastal Region (GA, FL, SC, NC) for Fellowship of Christian Athletes

I have known John Crosby since the day he gave his life to Christ. Since then he has made a life-changing impact for Christ because of his commitment to ministering to people in the business sector of our community. I'm sure as you read this book his insight will impact you as well.

**Cam Huxford**, Pastor, Savannah Christian Church

John Crosby is not only called, he is qualified to lead. Knowing John personally and understanding his life B.C. (before Christ), John brings a wealth of real life experience to the table. Agreeing to help lead a Bible study in a prominent workplace in Savannah, GA gave me a firsthand glimpse of his heart for workplace ministry. His approach and techniques are proven and effective. You will be blessed by this strong tool that you now hold in your hand!

**Brian Jobe**, Senior Pastor, Harvester Christian Church, Saint Charles, MO

# CONTENTS

# FOREWORD

In life and ministry it would be difficult to overestimate the value of focus. One of the trivial pursuits of my life is shooting sporting clays. In that sport the ability to focus not just on the target . . . but on a specific part of the target means the difference between success and failure. The value of focus in ministry is much greater . . . and more specific.

The ability to prevail in ministry requires that we focus on a number of targets at the same time. If our desire is to "lead with diligence" there is a compelling need to maintain a growing relationship with the Lord Jesus while at the same time investing in people, speaking encouraging words, growing in ministry skills, reading widely and thinking strategically.

*Called to Shepherd* is designed to help church leaders focus their hearts on the multiple priorities of life-changing ministry. As "iron sharpens iron" these devotions will sharpen your focus on ministry and inspire greater diligence as we pursue the greatest work in the world. I pray these thoughts will bless you . . . and empower you to bless others.

Cam Huxford,
Pastor, Savannah Christian Church

# CALLED TO . . .

L eadership is first and foremost a calling. God chose you to lead and has entrusted you with opportunities, resources, and relationships. Your primary responsibility as a leader is to wisely steward that which God has entrusted to you. The Called To series is intended to assist you in developing this wise stewardship by providing specific groups of leaders with biblical insight into specific leadership arenas and challenging you to align your lives and leadership with God's Word.

Each book in the *Called To* series is written in a weekly devotional format intended to give the reader:

- one biblical principle or challenge
- the time to pray and perhaps discuss the principle

- the opportunity to focus on that principle for a week, trusting God to provide opportunities to see that principle at work within the week

In my ministry serving leaders, this combination of reading, praying, discussing, and seeking to discern one principle each week throughout the year has proven to be an effective approach to developing wise leaders. I trust you will find this series to be an effective tool in your pursuit of honoring the God who called you to lead.

Lead wisely,
John Crosby

# INTRODUCTION

Twenty years ago, I left the beer business, a world I knew well, to enter the alien world of seminary. Surrounded by peers and professors much smarter and deeper than myself, I experienced almost overwhelming intimidation for the first time in my life. Certainly, I never thought I would write a book for pastors and ministry leaders. Fortunately, I discovered that the size of the hearts of these ministers and soon-to-be ministers was much greater than the size of their heads. My family and I were loved, nurtured, coached, and served by an extraordinary community of pastors and ministry leaders committed to honoring God through their lives and ministries. The names of pastors and ministry leaders who have influenced me are far too many to even attempt to list.

I have invested the last twenty years in biblical leadership development in churches, businesses, non-profits, and schools. I have written, taught, preached, coached, and consulted with leaders each week for most of those years. Yet I have never been bold enough to write a book for pastors and ministry leaders until now. One simple, genuine prayer led me to sit before my computer one afternoon and start writing this book. My desire was to express gratitude for what you do, but not to simply say "thank you." God has spoken to me so clearly through his leaders so often that I hoped he would offer something worthwhile to his chosen leaders through me.

That is the intention of this collection of leadership-oriented devotions for pastors and ministry leaders –to offer something of value from God to you. It is my deepest hope that the words in this book will reflect, not my personality or opinions, but God's Word to you. I know that you have more to read than you care to think about. I know the value of your time. That is why these are brief, weekly devotions. Years of discipling smart, busy, no-nonsense leaders have taught me to present biblical leadership principles in a weekly, concise, sometimes hard-hitting manner, asking leaders to pray and discuss the principle, and to simply ask God to reveal the principle at work the following week. You will not find deep theology or warm, feel-good expressions within these pages. Yet, you may realize God has a simple message here specifically for you that will exponentially enhance your leadership.

Lead wisely,
John Crosby

# THE BEST MINISTRY PREPARATION

*Brothers, think of what you were when you were called. Not many of you were wise by human standards; not many were influential; not many were of noble birth. But God chose the foolish things of the world to shame the wise; God chose the weak things of the world to shame the strong.*

**1 Corinthians 1:26-27**

Some pastors just can't seem to let go of their past. If you listen carefully, it's clear that they think their past was THE best preparation they have for ministry. Perhaps they can better understand thieves, alcoholics, or addictions because of their former lives. Maybe they have extraordinary business experience, or they are sixth generation pastors. Pride takes many forms.

If we understand God's plan for our lives, we know that he clearly uses the best, worst, and everything in-between for his glory. Certainly he uses the experiences of our past to shape our ministries. God delights in taking what Satan and the world have done in our lives and bringing about life and joy. The cross, the most barbaric of Roman execution tools, becoming the symbol of Christianity is the best example of that.

However, THE best ministry preparation has nothing to do with who we were before we were called. THE best ministry preparation is the work of the Holy Spirit on and in our lives. God chose us, not because of who we were, but because of what he could do through us.

How are you clouding his work with your testimony?

# COMPLETING, NOT COMPETING

*Is Christ divided? Was Paul crucified for you? Were you
baptized into the name of Paul?*

**1 Corinthians 1:13**

Pastors are leaders, and leaders tend to be competitors by
nature. The most natural thing in the world is to look
around at other pastors, churches, and ministries and com-
pare what you are doing to what they are doing. Who has
the biggest numbers? The best facilities? The coolest music?
Certainly, comparisons for the sake of improvement are wise.
But do your comparisons stop there? It is so easy for our
competitive nature to creep into rating one another.

When it comes to matters of importance, competition
breeds division. And what could be more important than
kingdom matters? The world offers enough division. Why

are we, who are in Christ, divided? When it comes to one another, God calls us to complete, not compete.

Are you harboring jealousy toward another pastor or ministry? Be honest. Do you find yourself prideful or defensive when discussing other ministries? You'd be wise to come clean with God and an accountability partner and repent. Nothing has the potential to undermine your ministry like pride and fear.

# STEWARDS FIRST

*So then, men ought to regard us as servants of Christ, and as those entrusted with the secret things of God.*

**1 Corinthians 4:1**

Answering the call to pastor a church is, in many ways, agreeing to a life full of apparent paradoxes. Applicants are asked to submit video examples of dynamic, engaging preaching. Committees seek to interview the most inspiring and visionary leaders. The expectation is clear—we need a captain for our ship! But Paul gives us a very different picture in the above verse. He says that pastors should be seen as servants. In fact, the word we translate "servants" literally meant "under-rowers." This word referred to the slaves who were kept below deck and rowed the huge Roman galleys.

How do we reconcile these apparent contradictions? It is helpful to remember that Paul was talking about himself and Apollos, two of the most educated, well-known, and visionary pastors in the history of the church. Paul is suggesting that respect for the steward never exceeds respect for the master. The Corinthian church had become so enamored with their leaders, past and present, that they were failing to be respectful and obedient to their master. Regardless of gifts, talents, education, experience . . . the only value a pastor brings to the church is in how he uses what he has been given to serve his master.

Pastors are first and foremost stewards. Regardless of where, when, or what we are doing, we are to steward that which has been given to us in a manner that pleases our master. Consider the last forty-eight hours. Who have you sought to please? What would the rest of this week look like if you clearly sought to be a wise steward, pleasing your master?

# THE MOST DANGEROUS PATH

*My conscience is clear, but that does not make me innocent. It is the Lord who judges me.*

**1 Corinthians 4:4**

Have you ever noticed how quickly a clear conscience can become a self-righteous attitude? We hear about someone doing something that we would not dare do, and suddenly we are swinging the judge's gavel. We often prioritize sin, making the sins of another somehow darker or more sinister than our own sin. Perhaps, at any given moment, we may think ourselves free from temptation or sin. But our clear conscience does not make us innocent. We may be viewed and respected as the most spiritually mature or "above reproach" leaders in our community. But God needs neither the community nor us to testify on our behalf.

There is such a thin line between a clear conscience and a self-righteous attitude. It is when we are least convicted about the sin in our own lives that we walk the most dangerous path.

# WHY DO YOU BOAST?

*For who makes you different from anyone else? What do you have that you did not receive? And if you did receive it, why do you boast as if you did not?*

**1 Corinthians 4:7**

Have you ever noticed how some leaders get a title and act like they have arrived? They are *given* a leadership role, and they assume they are at the top of the pyramid with everyone there below them waiting to somehow serve them, as if they have some newfound rights.

While the world often embraces the privileges and rewards of leadership, Scripture teaches that leadership is a gift. We are *given* leadership opportunities. Wise leaders understand that leadership is less about rights and more about responsibilities. The more people we are entrusted to lead, the more people we are responsible to serve. The reward for faithful leadership is usually more responsibility to serve more people. As leaders, we tread on dangerous ground when anything other than honoring God through the wise stewardship of the relationships, resources, strengths, gifts, talents, opportunities, and time he provides motivates us to lead.

# WALK STEADFASTLY INTO THE ARENA

*For it seems to me that God has put us apostles on display at the end of the procession, like men condemned to die in the arena. We have been made a spectacle to the whole universe, to the angels as well as to men.*

**1 Corinthians 4:9**

When the Romans conquered new lands, they divided many of the defeated men into three categories. First, they took many captured warriors to Rome. These trained fighters were led into the Coliseum to entertain the Roman citizens by fighting to the death as gladiators. The second group was the able-bodied, non-military men. These men were usually sold and distributed as slaves. Finally, the remaining old, feeble, lame, sick, or otherwise disabled men were led at the end of a procession into the arena, following the gladiator fights, to face whatever beasts the Romans thought would provide entertainment ripping these men apart. Not much was expected from these men. Those who resisted were usually killed before entering the Coliseum, so it took courage just to enter the Coliseum with everyone simply expecting them to be savagely killed.

It is this third group to which Paul is comparing pastors. Ask any police officer what the most dangerous kind of call is, and you will most likely be told "domestic calls." Yet, is that not precisely where pastors make their living? Pastors live and work in the midst of relational crises. Pastors knowingly walk into the most hopeless of situations.

The difference between courage and foolishness is faith. For a person to assume the role and responsibilities of a pastor, walking into the most hopeless of situations without a rich and growing faith in the One who brings hope and light into the darkest of situations is simply foolishness. When the world views you as a spectacle and your efforts as vain or useless, walk steadfastly into the arena, knowing it is our God who calls you.

# A FATHER'S ROLE

*What do you prefer? Shall I come to you with a whip, or in love and with a gentle spirit?*

**1 Corinthians 4:21**

My wife recently called me to tell me that one of my three teenagers, who is bigger than my wife, refused to cooperate with her wishes. I asked her to give the disobedient teen the phone and proceeded to remind my unruly son that I was coming home and he would choose my mood by the way he responded to his mother.

Good fathers understand that no matter how distasteful disciplining your children is, firm accountability is an essential part of a healthy family. In 1 Corinthians 4, Paul indicates that part of the responsibility of being a pastor is serving as a father, not *the* father (that's a cult!), but a father.

Good fathers are motivated by love. They protect, model, guide, teach, encourage, and provide accountability for the members of the family. Good fathers also understand that only accountability enveloped in love, humility, and options will have a lasting impact.

Are you avoiding your responsibilities as a pastor? If you're willing to hold people accountable for their actions, are you just as willing to do so in love and humility? Are you allowing people the opportunity to respond?

# LEADINGTHEFLOCK

*I tell you the truth, the man who does not enter the sheep pen by the gate, but climbs in by some other way, is a thief and a robber. The man who enters by the gate is the shepherd of his sheep. The watchman opens the gate for him, and the sheep listen to his voice. He calls his own sheep by name and leads them out. When he has brought out all his own, he goes on ahead of them, and his sheep follow him because they know his voice. But they will never follow a stranger; in fact, they will run away from him because they do not recognize a stranger's voice.*

**John 10:1-5**

The way of the shepherd was simple. At night, the shepherds would gather their flocks together in an area enclosed by rock walls with shepherds rotating the duties of watchman through the night. The following morning, each shepherd would call his sheep by name and lead them to water and pastures.

Those who know sheep understand that Jesus did not randomly choose this animal to describe God's people. Neither did he choose them simply out of convenience. Sheep are interesting animals. Unlike cows, horses, hogs, or other livestock, sheep cannot be driven. You're in for a long day should you decide to get behind sheep and force them in a given direction. Sheep follow only the one with whom they have established trust.

Sound familiar? If it does not, it will. As an excited visionary ministry leader, you may see ten years ahead of everyone else. You may have a great plan, and the steps may be logical and realistic. But if you have not established trust, if your people do not believe that you care about them, you will fail. Hope, clarity, competence, stability, and discipline are essential to ministry success, but, as priorities, they fall far behind trust and compassion.

Are you getting resistance to what seems so right? Could it be that you need to slow down and deepen relationships? Confrontation never relieves fear, but trust and compassion eventually do.

# TRUST

*Jesus answered, "I am the way and the truth and the life."*

**John 14:6**

Trust is the most fundamental leadership need. With it, a pastor can overcome many obstacles and shortcomings. Without trust, little else matters. Throughout the New Testament, Jesus began his teaching by saying *I tell you the truth.* The Gospel of John gave Jesus' purpose as coming to testify to *the truth.* Jesus actually claimed to be *the Truth.* The Holy Spirit was introduced and described by Jesus as the *Spirit of Truth.* On the other hand, Satan is commonly referred to as *the father of lies* and *the Deceiver.*

The surest way to be a trusted leader begins with knowing and following the One who is described within the

Word of God as *the Truth*. Building trust means first knowing truth and being trustworthy, then investing enough time into relationships that people see the real you. This is clear, simple, and undeniable. Yet it's not what most leaders want to hear. We'd much rather seek shortcuts. Americans in particular spend countless hours and resources on trust-building exercises, excursions, discussions, and trainings, most often with little to no long-term benefit.

Gallup's research on teams found that the most successful teams talked very little about trust, while the topic of trust dominated the conversations of struggling teams. Why? Because *building trust is not a competence. Building relationships is.* Trust, respect, integrity, and honesty are developed and revealed through strong relationships.

*Encouraging relationships flat-out trumps competence in building trust.*

- So what does this tell us about our approach to ministry?

- Are we building relationships or fruitlessly attempting to build trust?

- How do we develop a culture of trust within our ministry?

# GAINING WISDOM

*If any of you lacks wisdom, he should ask God, who gives generously to all without finding fault, and it will be given to him.*

**James 1:5**

When the Bible speaks of wisdom, it is referring to God's perspective. To gain wisdom is to gain God's perspective. I love the sarcasm in James' writing: *If any of you lacks wisdom . . .* Clearly, we each lack wisdom. Proverbs 1:7 says *Fear of the Lord is the beginning of wisdom.* Each passage is pointing to humility as the beginning of wisdom. James says I must first acknowledge that I lack wisdom before I can gain wisdom. I must acknowledge that I don't have all the answers, that I don't even have all the questions. Fear of the Lord is that recognition that there is a God, and I am not him.

The great news in the verse above is that when I realize I need God's perspective on my job, my spouse, my life, my circumstances . . . I simply need to ask, not for God to fill my prescription for solving my problems, but for him to show me his perspective. There are no hoops, no mantras, no minimal requirements, because God knows when we see the gap between our lives and his will, wisdom always brings its own conviction.

Do you have the humility and courage to ask God to reveal his perspective on the most troubling areas of your life?

# HYDRATE

*On the last and greatest day of the Feast, Jesus stood and said in a loud voice, "If anyone is thirsty, let him come to me and drink. Whoever believes in me, as the Scripture has said, streams of living water will flow from within him." By this he meant the Spirit, whom those who believed in him were later to receive.*

**John 7:37-39**

How important is it for your ministry to stay hydrated? Every athlete worth his salt knows hydration is crucial to performance. Even the best game-changers will fall short of expectations if they get dehydrated. We have each watched as the dehydration of a key athlete jeopardized the whole outcome of a competition.

If the outcome of a competition is at risk when an athlete dehydrates, how much more is at risk when a pastor dehydrates? We have been entrusted with sharing God's Word and reflecting his love and grace through our ministries. God trusts us with his children, and he empowers us with his Spirit. When we spend time in his Word and in prayer, he hydrates us, preparing us for anything our opposition can offer. When we lose interest in him and make excuses, we compromise his trust and enter the game unsteady, unclear, weak, and vulnerable. If you take leading the flock seriously, make it a point never to address your people before getting hydrated.

# IRON SHARPENS IRON

*As iron sharpens iron, so one man sharpens another.*

**Proverbs 27:17**

Everyone wants to succeed, but few people structure for success. We want the benefits without the work, rewards without challenges, and recognition before goals are even met. Solomon gives us a crucial element of success in this verse. It is a focused, Christ-centered relationship with a peer.

You could put an attorney, a pastor, and a farmer in an accountability group, and each could consistently make excuses for falling short of expectations by suggesting that the others did not understand the demands of his life. However, put two or three pastors–who see each other as equals, trust one another, understand each other's work, and perhaps know each others' spouses and children—together in an accountability group, and it opens a whole new world of transparency, accountability, support, affirmation, correction, and friendship. According to Solomon, a peer who is willing to open God's Word with you to give and receive advice, counsel, and correction is one of the best prescriptions for success.

Perhaps it's time to find another pastor to join you in an *iron sharpening iron* relationship.

# THE BIG KAHUNA

*Recklesswordspiercelikeasword,butthetongueofthe wise brings healing.*

**Proverbs 12:18**

Take a minute and reflect on your ministry. Which pastor had the greatest influence on your ministry? I'm betting the "Big Kahuna" was not necessarily the most educated or gifted pastor you knew. He (or she) was a leader who weighed his words wisely. He understood that criticism, cynicism, and sarcasm weigh much more than words of affirmation, encouragement, and insight. He saw potential in you and sought to bring it out, using accountability to build you up rather than tear you down.

Leadership matters, and the words of a pastor carry tremendous weight. Wise leaders weigh their words wisely.

Now, you're the Big Kahuna in someone else's eyes. You have been entrusted with people to lead and opportunities to build those people up. What the Big Kahuna says carries tremendous weight in the lives of your followers. You have the power to build up, to heal, to tear down, and to pierce. Weigh your words wisely, leaving your people walking taller than when you arrived.

# AND THEN SOME

*Suppose one of you had a servant plowing or looking after the sheep. Would he say to the servant when he comes in from the field, "Come along now and sit down to eat"? Would he not rather say, "Prepare my supper, get yourself ready and wait on me while I eat and drink; after that you may eat and drink"? Would he thank the servant because he did what he was told to do? So you also, when you have done everything you were told to do, should say, "We are unworthy servants; we have only done our duty."*

**Luke 17:7-10**

Few people would consider doing only what is required as a character flaw, but the Bible says otherwise. Most people fall into one of two categories: Those who *do just enough* and those who complete what is required *and then some*. The first group does *just enough* to get by, *just enough* to get paid, *just enough* to avoid getting fired. The second group is not necessarily smarter or more talented, but they consistently exceed expectations—out working, out thinking, and out smarting others—simply doing what others are unwilling to do, say, learn, or risk. According to Jesus, if we do only what we are required to do, our performance is nothing special and is unworthy of reward. If you want to build a team that goes "the extra mile," it starts with modeling an *and then some* attitude.

# STRONG, ENDURING MINISTRY

*If a house is divided against itself, that house cannot stand.*

**Mark 3:25**

Is there anything worse than a ministry that is strangled by dissension? It chokes any sense of accomplishment right out of the ministry. There is no substitute for unity. It is absolutely essential for any sustainable ministry.

The key word is "sustainable." Are you simply looking to get through the pending budget process or current firestorm? Or are you seeking to build an enduring ministry? A good minister can manage the ins and outs of a fragmented ministry to achieve some short-term impact. But it takes a leader with the appropriate skills and courage to overcome dissension and build an enduring ministry.

Unity is not about eliminating conflict. Indeed, every strong, enduring ministry is comprised of members with different strengths and perspectives. When differences are focused on issues and are addressed openly, clearly, and respectfully among the team, they often bring the strongest resolutions. Yet, when members turn the conflicts into quarrels by making them personal, a wise leader knows his "house is divided against itself," and the parties must be addressed.

# MOVING FORWARD

*Brothers, I do not consider myself yet to have taken hold of it. But one thing I do: Forgetting what is behind and straining toward what is ahead, I press on toward the goal to win the prize for which God has called me heavenward in Christ Jesus.*

**Philippians 3:13-14**

What happens when a pastor mistakes one big success for a successful career? When we assume that one success will propel us to future success, we often fail to adequately prepare for the opportunities and challenges before us. Great victories bring more focused opposition, which requires more focused preparation. Also, God tends to reward success with bigger challenges.

When a Christian leader relies on the stories, testimonies, and lessons from his past to prepare him for the opportunities before him, he often finds himself lacking the wisdom and influence needed to help those he has been entrusted to lead. The Apostle Paul never got so enamored with one success that he forgot to prepare for the next challenge. His example is to avoid resting on the successes of yesterday and to strain forward, preparing for what is ahead. Are you serious about leading the flock? Are you pressing forward in your desire to honor God? Are you spending enough time in Scripture and prayer to prepare for whatever lies ahead?

# FIRST FORGIVE

*Therefore, if you are offering your gift at the altar and there remember that your brother has something against you, leave your gift there in front of the altar. First go and be reconciled to your brother, then come and offer your gift.*

**Matthew 5:23-24**

For most of the leaders I serve, this is the most significant character flaw I see. Leaders tend to be competitive. Yet competitive people tend to hold grudges. We begrudge former staff for leaving our organization; we resent critical members and family members who don't support or appreciate our sacrifices; we get peeved when a friend supports another ministry more than ours. Some of these issues we attempt to reconcile, and some we just think we'll take to the grave.

Few things have the potential to undermine and thwart a pastor's attempt to positively influence others like a bitter heart.

STOP. *If you're breaking down the above passage and pointing out that if the other person does not know about your anger then he can't hold it against you . . .* just stop. You're missing the point! Anger is like weed seeds. Spread a few in your yard and see what happens. When anger takes root, sin takes hold. Anger will choke the joy right out of your life. God values your obedience FAR MORE than your worship and/or ministry activity. That's why he says stop and reconcile BEFORE worshipping.

Perhaps you need to put this devotion down right now, swallow your pride, and make a tough phone call or–even better—*man-up (or woman-up)* and go reconcile with someone in person. I'm pleading with you.

If someone has come to mind while reading this, don't try to determine *if* you should address the situation. Trust the Holy Spirit and take care of business. I know of nothing more personally freeing and blessed more often by God than when we extend forgiveness and reconcile with others. I can promise you this–when you truly forgive the person you least wish to forgive, your load will be lightened more than you expect. It always is when we follow Christ. Indeed, what could be more Christ-like than going the extra mile and extending forgiveness, even to someone who may not deserve your forgiveness?

# PASSION AND PURPOSE

*Folly delights a man who lacks judgment, but a man of understanding keeps a straight course.*

**Proverbs 15:21**

Godly people recognize leadership as a calling. They recognize that God has entrusted them with opportunities to lead and he expects them to wisely steward everything he entrusts to them. Leadership is a calling which should never be taken lightly.

Leaders who lack passion and purpose are easily distracted. Passion and purpose keep the leader and those he has been entrusted to lead away from "folly" and on a "straight course." Are your passion and purpose clear? Do others align themselves easily with your direction? If not, perhaps it is time to quietly and intentionally rethink your direction, asking God for his direction.

# YOUR INNER CIRCLE

*"My soul is overwhelmed with sorrow to the point of death. Stay here and keep watch with me."*

**Matthew 26:38**

Pause a minute and think about the words above. Jesus, the Alpha and the Omega, was asking his friends to help him with an emotional struggle. It's amazing to me that the greatest leader of all time would show such vulnerability.

A pastor who keeps everyone at arm's length never optimizes his potential. No matter how important and high profile we become, we need an inner circle of friends whom we can call upon in emotional struggles. I have often watched strong, talented leaders leave ministries short of their goals, largely because they never really developed close relationships with the people around them.

Jesus concentrated much of his energy on befriending and developing a small inner circle of people he led. He knew that when his inner circle gained his insight and inspiration, it would exponentially increase his impact. This kind of reaching influence is seldom achieved through staff meetings and simply working together. Jesus shared life with his inner circle. He served them and called upon them for help.

Pride and fear lead us to withdraw from people when we need them the most. You cannot lead from isolation. Spending time alone with God and with crowds while avoiding close personal relationships with your team is not the ministry Jesus modeled for us. Are you following him or not?

# GRASSHOPPERS IN OUR OWN EYES

*The land we explored devoured those living in it. All the people we saw there are of great size . . . We seemed like grasshoppers in our own eyes, and we looked the same to them.*

**Numbers 13:32-33**

Y ou've seen it. You work hard to prepare your team. You have succeeded at increasingly complex challenges. Then the big opportunity arrives, an opportunity the size of which you have only dreamed. The eyes of your team members are as big as saucers. They are overwhelmed. Perhaps it's the budget. Maybe it's the visibility, or just the sheer number of obstacles. But deep down, you know—your team members are grasshoppers in their own eyes. The potential obstacles have thwarted them before they even started.

For vast numbers of Americans, life has become staggeringly easy–and incredibly unfulfilling. We have empowered people to perfect the art of avoiding any real challenge. Life in modern society is designed to eliminate as many unforeseen events as possible, and as inviting as that seems, it leaves people hopelessly unfulfilled and bored. If we allow shallow excuses rather than heightened performances when facing overwhelming odds, we destine our team members to lives of mediocrity.

As pastors, we must recognize the magnitude of what we have been entrusted to do. It is when we are most overwhelmed that we see God work in unmistakable ways. As my pastor once told me, "You will never know the power of the Holy Spirit in your preaching until you preach when you have neither the energy nor the desire to do so." The greatest challenges in the lives of your people are hardly challenging to our Father in heaven. But it is only in experiencing his grace, peace, and power within those challenges that we truly begin to understand his love for us.

# FROM LION TO LOAF

*For these commands are a lamp, this teaching is a light, and the corrections of discipline are the way to life, keeping you from the immoral woman, from the smooth tongue of the wayward wife. Do not lust in your heart after her beauty or let her captivate you with her eyes, for the prostitute reduces you to a loaf of bread, and the adulteress preys upon your very life.*

**Proverbs 6:23-26**

M ost leaders are like lions. They want to rule their domain. They are bold, courageous, and forward thinking. No one need go before them. They will blaze their own trails and write their own stories. They earn and expect respect. Their fears are few and rarely revealed. A good leader is seldom distracted from a well-prepared plan. But the beauty, smooth tongue, and captivating eyes of a wayward wife have reduced many to a loaf of bread.

Don't fool yourself. It's not a matter of if you have this weakness, but of how you prepare for it. Be on guard. If you are more relaxed or casual about honoring and protecting your marriage than you are about following your ministry routine, you're headed for the oven.

# WORTH YOUR SALT

*You are the salt of the earth. But if the salt loses its saltiness, how can it be made salty again? It is no longer good for anything, except to be thrown out and trampled by men.*

**Matthew 5:13**

I love wrestling. In fact, anyone who spends significant time with me hears about weight classes, tournaments, brackets, pins, camps . . . I don't try to recruit my friends to wrestle. I don't seek to teach them wrestling moves. I don't even plan to talk about wrestling. It just comes out. I'm passionate about wrestling, and it just comes out in conversations in every area of my life. I don't even have to initiate wrestling conversations. Once people know my passion, it is the most natural thing in the world for them to ask me about my passion. I'm guessing you're just as passionate about something, and that passion seasons many of your conversations.

That's exactly what Jesus meant when he said that we are the salt of the earth. Our love for him and our gratitude for what he did should season every area of our lives. You may passionately preach or teach the gospel during the prescribed times, but what about the conversations in your neighborhood or at the gym? You have been given an extraordinary gift, and you are expected to be passionately grateful. When we love the Lord our God with all our heart, all our soul, and all our mind, that passion comes out in every area of our lives. People who know us know our passions. We don't have to preach, teach, judge, or "evangelize." When our passion is clear, people will ask about it.

How often do people ask about your passion? When is the last time that someone outside your church asked you about Jesus?

# THE CHINESE BAMBOO TREE

*Brothers, I could not address you as spiritual but as worldly—mere infants in Christ. I gave you milk, not solid food, for you were not yet ready for it. Indeed, you are still not ready. You are still worldly. For since there is jealousy and quarreling among you, are you not worldly?*

**1 Corinthians 3:1-3**

C an you identify with Paul? Have you poured yourself into your ministry, only to find people arguing, fighting, or acting immaturely? Take heart. Even the Apostle Paul experienced great struggles while seeking to develop people.

If you were called to pastor, you have been trusted to develop people. Some people will show signs of growth early. Others may not seem to be growing at all. Consider the Chinese bamboo tree. This remarkable tree shows no outward signs of growth until its fifth year. You plant the bulb and water a small shoot for four years while seeing absolutely no growth. However, growth is taking place. This tiny tree spends four years developing an enormous network of underground roots. In fact, your strongest team members would find it nearly impossible to yank, jerk, twist, or tug this tiny four-year-old tree out of the ground. Then, in its fifth year, this tiny tree with an enormous root system erupts into a staggering height of eighty feet.

Keep planting and watering. You have no idea what God is doing below the surface. Trust him to provide the growth. He may not choose to work on our timetable, but he always uses what we make available.

# FOLLOW WHOLEHEARTEDLY

*But my brothers who went up with me made the hearts of the people melt with fear. I, however, followed the Lord my God wholeheartedly. So on that day Moses swore to me, "The land on which your feet have walked will be your inheritance and that of your children forever, because you have followed the Lord my God wholeheartedly."*

**Joshua 14:8-9**

Caleb was an extraordinary leader. He was one of the twelve spies Moses sent into the Promised Land. His report was full of anticipation and confidence. He was ready to take the land. But he was out-voted ten to two. He stood his ground and nobly argued what he correctly discerned was God's calling. Yet, fear led the people to reject his desire to take the land. The price of their fear was severe–forty years wandering in the desert.

Caleb adjusted his course, suffering alongside those he was entrusted to lead. But he never abandoned his passion or his purpose. Nearly forty-five years later, at age eighty-five, Caleb was rewarded with the very land he wished to take from the "giants" who caused so much fear.

Passion and purpose are transcendent. Caleb found both in following the Lord wholeheartedly. Pastors who do so have far more growth, enthusiasm, and unity than others. But it can't be faked, and it does not come without costs. Will you follow God wholeheartedly when others shy away? God always rewards the kind of wholehearted, patient, steadfast purpose and passion demonstrated by Caleb.

# KEEPINGYOUROATH

*He who keeps his oath even when it hurts . . . will never be shaken.*

**Psalms 15:4b**

Be honest. When is the last time you made a casual commitment that you never intended to keep?

"I'll call you later."

"I'll look into that."

"We'll do so next time."

Is it possible that your word meant a lot more to someone else than it did to you? Or perhaps you made a commitment that you fully intended to keep, but "things changed." It's interesting what kinds of things we can find more valuable than our word: convenience, acceptance, pride, finances . . .

"Keeping your oath even when it hurts" means that you'll do *what* you said you'll do, *when* you said you'd do it, and *how* you said you'd do it, even if it becomes more costly, inconvenient, or time-consuming than you planned. A friend of mine, whose grandfather was sheriff of a nearby county for many years, said his grandfather taught him to make as few promises as possible and to keep every one. That's good advice.

# TIME THIEVES

*Moses' father-in-law replied, "What you are doing is not good. You and these people who come to you will only wear yourselves out. The work is too heavy for you; you cannot handle it alone."*

**Exodus 18:17-18**

Every pastor understands the need to prioritize responsibilities. But what do you do next? What do you do after you have identified what matters most?

The next step is to identify what you must stop doing in order to do what matters most. Time is your only irreplaceable asset. When an hour or a day is gone, it is gone. We each have less time ahead of us now than we had last week. This makes identifying the things that interfere with us doing what matters most absolutely critical. Before you begin adding tasks to an already blossoming "to-do" list, most of us need to create a "stop-doing" list. We need to identify the convenient, tough, urgent, easy, enjoyable, fearful, or prideful issues that steal our time and keep us from accomplishing what matters most. Our unidentified time thieves are robbing us blind!

In Exodus 18:13-26, we're told that Moses sat "from morning till evening" as he attempted to settle each of the disputes among his two million followers. His father-in-law, Jethro, saw this and challenged Moses. He said the workload was too heavy, preventing Moses from working wisely and wearing both Moses and the people out (imagine waiting for your turn in court in a single line with thousands of others). Jethro told Moses how to delegate the work to satisfy the people and relieve the personal strain, freeing Moses to lead wisely.

To keep improving our leadership, we must continually discern between mere activity and actual accomplishment. Doing the wrong things well thwarts many would-be leaders. Take out your calendar, your to-do lists, and your reflections of the last few days. What is stealing your time? What needs to be on your stop-doing list?

# LEAVING A LEGACY

*There is no remembrance of men of old, and even those who are yet to come will not be remembered by those who follow.*

**Ecclesiastes 1:11**

What really ignites your passion? What keeps you up at night? Is it your desire to make a difference? Is it your hope to leave a legacy? We love thinking big. We love to look years ahead at what we hope to build, what we'll be remembered for. But Solomon says, "You're mistaken. You're only dreaming. What you do won't matter."

Solomon is really referring to the audacious, noble, well-intended, prideful goals that we think WE can accomplish. He is suggesting that you and I, like him, think far too highly of ourselves, that we give ourselves far more credit than we deserve, and we over-estimate our contributions to our communities.

Our giftedness, strategic thinking, education, experience, influence, passion, hard work, commitment, and win-loss records will all be eventually forgotten apart from how God chooses to use us. God is looking to shape history with humble people with a spirit of dependence and a subjection to his authority. Just look at Abraham, Moses, Gideon, David, or the twelve disciples. They were "nobodies" in terms of nobility, appearance, and abilities, but God loved their hearts and used them to shape history. God would rather use a humble nobody than a prideful "ten-talent" guy to make a lasting impression.

When you bring humility and obedience to the game, God shapes you to shape history. When you don't, little else matters.

# GENUINE PRAYERS

*Your Father knows what you need before you ask him.*

**Matthew 6:8**

Most of us have neutered our prayers. We've been taught to pray politely and respectfully, perhaps even rhythmically. God seems to want something more genuine. He wants our words to him to reflect our true feelings. He yearns for our prayers to resemble our conversations with our best friends rather than our prepared messages from behind the pulpit.

Have you ever really "taken off the gloves" and expressed your most painful feelings and questions to God in prayer? He already knows what you're going through. He knows what you're thinking. Sharing anything short of your real feelings must seem awfully shallow or phony to the God who already knows your heart.

# LISTENING AND LEARNING

*Let the wise listen and add to their learning, and let the discerning get guidance.*

**Proverbs 1:5**

Ever notice how many young church planters have early success and then just seem to fade away? One of the trappings of success is reading and believing the headlines about ourselves. When we think we've arrived, we tend to stop listening and learning.

Biologists tell us that every living organism is either growing or dying. Pastors who lack intentional exposure to new thoughts and challenges may feel good about themselves, but make no mistake—their leadership is dying. Are you committed to personal and professional growth? What have you done in the last sixty days to stretch yourself? If you continue learning at your current pace, where will you be a year from now?

# KNOWN BY OUR ACTIONS

*Even a child is known by his actions, by whether his conduct is pure and right.*

**Proverbs 20:11**

I know it's cliché, but actions speak louder than words. What we do says far more about us than what we say. It's easy to quote Bible verses and season our conversations with religious language. We think we're letting our light shine by offering to pray for a friend going through tough times. But what happens five minutes later when that friend watches us chew someone out for "dropping the ball"? What are we telling those we have been entrusted to lead about Christianity when we preach great messages, and then they hear us lie and gossip?

Don't kid yourself. People watch Christians in leadership. They may not say anything when your actions align with your words. But they definitely notice when your actions deviate from what you claim.

God does not expect perfection. No one is perfect. But you don't want your carelessness to come between someone else and God. Don't let your mouth or your careless actions undermine your opportunity to make a Kingdom impact.

# WORTHY WORDS AND ACTIONS

*Whatever happens, conduct yourselves in a manner worthy of the gospel of Christ.*

**Philippians 1:27**

Jesus gave his life so that we might live. He deserves our gratitude. He deserves our love. He deserves our respect and obedience. If we believe in his omnipresence, if we believe he is near at all times, if we believe he hears our every word and sees our every deed, if we have been entrusted to lead, how do we justify continually dishonoring him before others with careless words and deeds? Do reckless drivers and rude servers really warrant our inappropriate reactions? Really?

Leading the flock is about more than growing a ministry. Godly leadership shapes lives. The words and actions you choose speak volumes into the lives of those you influence.

James says teachers will be judged more strictly than others. It is hard to imagine a pastor who is not a teacher.

James also says that a salt spring cannot produce fresh water. In other words, your words and actions are indicators of your heart. You may have the resumé and the experience, but if your heart is not prepared for leadership, you will dishonor Christ through leading. What are you doing to prepare your heart for leadership? Are you investing time with God and in his Word?

# YOUR TEAM'S SWEET SPOT

*So the Twelve gathered all the disciples together and said, "It would not be right for us to neglect the ministry of the word of God in order to wait on tables . . .*

*We will turn this responsibility over to them and will give our attention to prayer and the ministry of the word."*

**Acts 6:2, 3b, 4**

What do you do well? What else are you doing? What are your team members doing? Are you holding onto responsibilities simply because you want them done right? The best teams are always built around strengths, passions, and needs. Pride and fear keep us from developing people around us and delegating responsibilities.

Your team's sweet spot will be found when each person finds the intersection of his strengths and passions and the ministry's needs. You know the needs. Do you know each person well enough to know their strengths and passions? Do you have the humility and courage to do so?

# THE SIZE OF THE FIGHT IN THE DOG

*We are therefore Christ's ambassadors, as though God were making his appeal through us.*

**2 Corinthians 5:20**

There are approximately 155 million regular church-goers in America. In other words, we have enough team members to have a much greater kingdom impact. Stop for a moment and let that sink in. Imagine the possibilities if every churchgoer took the call to be an ambassador for Christ seriously. As the old saying goes, "it is not the size of the dog in the fight, but the size of the fight in the dog" that matters.

The moral fabric of our nation is unraveling. We are increasingly and openly embracing unprecedented levels of sin, corruption, greed, and deceit. Unfortunately, each new generation will accept this tide of ungodliness as normal, *unless* trusted Christian leaders take their calling seriously and unashamedly, consistently honor their Lord and Savior.

God can choose to change the direction of our nation. But he has been clear that he will only do so through humble, godly leaders stepping forward and taking a stand. Who will issue that challenge? Who will model the way? You have been chosen for leadership. You have your people's undivided attention. You have opportunities to make a difference. You're already a "big dog." The question is "the size of the fight in the dog." As many have discovered, being an ambassador for Christ may not be an easy, convenient, politically-correct, or even socially acceptable calling. Surely, you won't call yourself a pastor and simply stay on the porch.

# STAND FIRM

*Therefore, my dear brothers, stand firm. Let nothing move you. Always give yourselves fully to the work of the Lord, because you know that your labor in the Lord is not in vain.*

**1 Corinthians 15:58**

Some weeks are just plain tough. There are days when each of us just wants to throw in the towel, wondering why we do what we do. Those are the days when the evil one begins to whisper words of self-doubt and despair. He wants us to think our work is in vain. He wants us to think we don't make a difference. He points to our team members who have embarrassed, disgraced, or worse. He points to the betrayals of others. He highlights our mistakes and shortcomings. He speaks through others both from afar and from within our inner circles. But the most dangerous voice is the one in our own heads: "This is a waste." "I am wasting my life." "This doesn't matter." "The whole world is against me."

You and I have been called to be obedient to the gospel, to follow Jesus, to be indwelt, empowered, and led by the Holy Spirit. We are called to honor the name of Jesus through our lives. What we do in the Lord is not in vain. We are not building a house simply to blow it up. We are not writing a paper simply to delete it. We are not making furniture simply to throw it in the fire. Leading the flock is a noble calling. You have been entrusted to shape the lives of those you lead. In positively influencing their lives, you are shaping the future of your community, our society, the church, and the kingdom. Scripture tells us that Jesus will complete what we have started in his name when he returns.

Your work matters to God. He is watching. Let him lead you. Let him empower you. When you honor him in the smallest of ways, you're building the kingdom. He will complete your work. He planted you right where you are. Stand firm. You matter.

# WISDOM IS SUPREME

*Wisdom is supreme; therefore get wisdom. Though it cost all you have, get understanding. Esteem her, and she will exalt you; embrace her, and she will honor you.*

**Proverbs 4:7-8**

Wisdom is God's perspective. It is seeing my circumstances, the people around me, my expectations, and the expectations of others as God sees them. For the leader who wishes to honor God, wisdom is without comparison. Solomon, whom the Bible says was the wisest man who ever lived, says "wisdom is supreme."

We gain wisdom through hearing, reading, and studying the Word of God. We also gain wisdom by seeking wise counsel and accountability from others committed to honoring God. During busy ministry times, some pastors decide that they are too busy to continue their personal time with God. We decide our preparation for teaching can serve as our quiet time, and we make excuses for not meeting with accountability partners.

Imagine a welder who wears his face shield until it's time to make a weld, a police officer who takes off his Kevlar vest to answer a domestic dispute, or a nurse who removes her glasses before drawing blood. If these examples seem silly, consider the pastor who stops seeking wisdom when he needs it most.

The God who called you to lead the flock will not abandon you. Why would you even consider abandoning him when you need him most? Lean into the Word and gain a clearer, more accurate perspective of the chaos around you, as well as a deeper sense of peace within you.

# POSING

*Simply let your "yes" be "yes" and your "no" "no"; anything beyond this comes from the evil one.*

**Matthew 5:37**

The ministry is full of posers. You know the type: "borrowing" the sermons of another; covering up their own liability to avoid consequences; pretending to be more spiritual than they are; misleading staff to think a promotion or a raise is closer than it is; offering excuses to hide reality; manipulating numbers to paint a favorable picture; omitting facts that reveal reality; misrepresenting experience.

Jesus reserved his harshest criticism for the posers of his day, the Pharisees, those leaders who claimed to be godly, but instead simply posed. Your ability to shape the lives of those you have been entrusted to lead will be directly proportional to your ability to be real with other people.

Playing the political game, straddling the fence, and telling people what you think they want to hear are just forms of posing. Jesus says soft, wishy-washy answers are from the evil one, and they eventually bring bitterness and resentment. Don't fall into this trap! If you cannot answer "yes" or "no," simply ask for time to think and pray about the issue and don't answer until your yes is yes or your no is no.

# KICKING BACK

*Come to me, all you who are weary and burdened, and I will give you rest. Take my yoke upon you and learn from me, for I am gentle and humble in heart, and you will find rest for your souls.*

**Matthew 11:28-29**

L eading the flock is a demanding responsibility. It's easy to feel pressured into working sixty to seventy hours per week. You address countless disputes, fret over difficult decisions, face unanswerable questions, deal with unbelievably critical people, and often lie awake in the middle of the night just staring at the ceiling.

Christianity is not about adding to that burden. Jesus does not want you to read his Word and speak to him out of obligation. He wants you to know him and enjoy his presence like a great cup of coffee, a well-worn jersey, your favorite fishing hole, or that hammock in the shade. He prepared for each day with a quiet conversation with his dad, and he eagerly welcomes you to join them.

Jesus actually promises to give us rest when we set aside our formal pretensions, take a deep breath, exhale, and chill with him. Your daily personal quiet time should be less about checklists and more about kicking back and learning from the guy who turned water to wine and cooked breakfast on the beach.

# POOR PERFORMERS

*But Paul did not think it wise to take him, because he had deserted them in Pamphylia and had not continued with them in the work.*

**Acts 15:38**

Some of a pastor's toughest decisions concern responding to poor staff performers. Consider the following steps when doing so:

PRAY—Ask God to give you his perspective on the performance and person.

Explore the 3Cs:

    1.   Is this a character issue?

    2.   Is this a competency issue?

    3.   Is this a chemistry issue?

Does this person *clearly understand* the roles, goals, responsibilities, and standards for this position?

Why is this person under-performing? Is it a lack of:

- training?
- motivation?
- experience?
- ability?
- clear assignment?

Consider your perspective. Instead of the old "I need to get rid of this person" mentality, consider this: Several biblical writers tell us that life is short. James says life is "but a vapor." When you appropriately release a person from a position in which he is failing, you are releasing him from that failure and freeing him to seek a role in which he can find success. Too many people are wasting their short lives in unfulfilling and unproductive jobs. With a proper release, it's even possible to instill in the person the excitement that comes from anticipating a new venture. It's not that this process will become easy. But the right perspective is one of releasing a person from failure to pursue something more fulfilling.

# WHEN WORDS ARE MANY

*When words are many, sin is not absent, but he who holds his tongue is wise.*

**Proverbs 10:19**

Think of a situation that you vowed never to repeat. We all have them. Chances are that someone spoke far too much.

Fools love to hear themselves talk. People who consider themselves above and beyond those listening also love to hear themselves talk. But where there is mutual respect, fewer words are needed, especially when facing a challenge.

My observation is that the leader sets the level of respect within his ministry. If the leader holds his tongue, his people will eventually follow suit. Are you setting the example you wish your team to follow? Are you choosing your words carefully?

# GOD'S CHARACTER

*But the fruit of the Spirit is love, joy, peace, patience, kindness, goodness, faithfulness, gentleness, and self-control.*

**Galatians 5:22**

Ever wrestle with the characteristics listed in Galatians 5:22? They are the personal characteristics of God. The Holy Spirit is the invisible presence of God, dwelling within every believer. If you have the Holy Spirit within you, which the Bible says every believer does, then you already have all of his characteristics within you. No one gets a partial dose.

The way to exhibit more peace, patience, or self-control is not to work harder at doing so. The Holy Spirit, living within you, already has these characteristics. If you want to exhibit more of God's character in and through your life, stop trying to manufacture the appearance and spend more time with the God you hope to reflect. The more you trust and submit to him, the more he will be seen in and through your life.

# FRESH BAKED COOKIES

*Taste and see that the Lord is good . . .*

**Psalm 34:8**

How did you approach this devotion? With enthusiasm, or out of a sense of obligation? How do you usually approach worship? Reading Scripture? Prayer?

We are among the busiest people in the history of the world. Few of us can function without some form of to-do lists, and most of us simply layer to-do lists over one another. We have to-do lists with personal necessities, then we add a layer of to-do lists with family or household needs, and then we add layers for ministry obligations and community expectations. Finally, we add a layer for matters of faith.

Jesus does not want to be approached as an obligation. He puts little value in checking Bible study, quiet time, preaching, committee meetings, or prayer off your list. Apart from knowing him better, our religious checklists are meaningless and counterproductive. Jesus wants a relationship with you. He wants his presence to be eagerly anticipated and celebrated, not simply considered or pondered. He wants to be approached less out of obligation and more like we'd approach a plate of fresh-baked cookies, brick-oven pizza, or a thick, juicy ribeye.

# IS IT BENEFICIAL?
# IS IT BINDING?

*Everything is permissible for me—but not everything is beneficial. Everything is permissible for me—but I will not be mastered by anything.*

**1 Corinthians 6:12**

There are far too many people fighting for "rights" without considering what is beneficial or binding. Only a fool will pursue that which is not beneficial or that which will bind or master him simply because he has the right to do so. Too many of us engage in activities which threaten to steal our influence, our careers, our marriages, or even our health, and yet we argue that it is our "right" to do so. We line up to exchange long-term peace and freedom for short-term pleasure.

God loves us. He wants us to experience peace and freedom. The Apostle Paul says that while we may have a legal right or it may be socially acceptable, we should remember that "You are not your own; you were bought at a price." To overlook what Jesus has done for us by engaging in that which will take our peace and freedom is foolishness.

# WHITE LIES

*Do not lie to each other, since you have taken off your old self with its practices and have put on the new self, which is being renewed in knowledge in the image of its creator.*

**Colossians 3:9-10**

I suppose some of you may feel belittled if I simply told you to tell the truth. Every person reading this knows the potential consequences of lying. But what about *white lies*? What about those times when we tell an assistant to tell someone we've left for the day to avoid a long, untimely conversation? Or when we tell an administrator we'll meet their deadline when we know we can't quite make it? Or when we suggest that we never received an e-mail that made an inconvenient request?

The Oxford Dictionary defines a *white lie* as "a harmless or trivial untruth." Most of us want to distinguish between our own white lies and "whoppers." But how does the Bible tell us to distinguish the difference? The Bible says there is no difference. In fact, the Bible warns us about categorizing or prioritizing sin of any kind. The Bible says there is no "trivial or harmless untruth." A lie is a lie.

As a pastor, you must recognize that people are watching and remembering far more about you than you realize. The integrity of your ministry will never exceed the integrity of your leadership. Each time your team members hear you lie, they understand that lying is acceptable in your ministry in certain circumstances. At that point, they will use their own judgment, not yours, about which circumstances justify lying.

# AREYOULISTENING?

*Hewhoanswersbeforelistening–thatishisfollyandhis
shame.*

**Proverbs 18:13**

*Afoolfindsnopleasureinunderstandingbutdelightsin
airing his own opinions.*

**Proverbs 18:2**

Most pastors invest vast amounts of energy developing
their own skills, such as ministry planning, preaching, understanding biblical languages, prioritizing responsibilities, delegation, and time-management. But sometimes,
we think experience neutralizes our need to listen. We've
been here, done that, got the t-shirt.

The Bible says that's just a foolish attitude. You and I will always learn more by listening than by speaking. We never outgrow the need to grow, and one of the most vital means of growth is listening. The most humbling experiences often follow those times when we think we have all the answers. Perhaps it's time to admit we neither have all the answers nor all the questions. Great ideas can come from the most unlikely of sources, if we're open to listening. Are *you* listening?

# SELECTINGLEADERS

*The Lord does not look at the things man looks at. Man looks at the outward appearance, but the Lord looks at the heart.*

**1 Samuel 16:7**

When sent to find the new king of Israel, Samuel first looked at the sons of Jesse just like everyone else did–from man's perspective. He expected to see the anointing of God through man's measurements. But God looks beyond physical size, talent, appearance, gifts, intellect, speed, strength, and everything else to peer into a man's heart.

When selecting leaders, we are always wise to follow God's approach. God always selects a person of character for leadership. Humility, obedience, and submission to God's authority are the cornerstones to God's selection process.

Popular opinion is irrelevant to God. He often sidelines those expected to succeed and does the extraordinary through the most ordinary of leaders because he is looking beyond outward appearances into the heart. Do you know your leaders well enough to know their hearts? Are you keeping those who have compromised their character in leadership roles for the wrong reasons? Compromised character leads to a compromised team.

# TRIPPING THE WEAK

*Be careful, however, that the exercise of your freedom*
*does not become a stumbling block to the weak.*

**1 Corinthians 8:9**

What is your personal vice? What's that one thing that you know some people object to you doing, but you do it anyway? Maybe it's drinking–the Bible does not forbid it. Maybe it's tobacco–it's your right to choose. Perhaps it's "slight" profanity–get over it.

Your vice is most likely legal, not prohibited in Scripture, and perhaps widely accepted among your friends and peers. But what about weaker, impressionable, or immature people who look to you as a Christian leader? Like it or not, pastors are in the business of influencing behavior. If you're somewhere people recognize you as a pastor, you're still influencing behavior. You may enjoy your vice, but does it align with the influence you hope to have and the legacy you hope to leave? We will each be held accountable for how we steward the opportunities given us. No one wants to be remembered for tripping the weak.

# SUCCESS

*Still other seed fell on good soil.*

**Mark 4:8**

Sometimes we simply use the wrong metrics. We see others leading people to confess Christ just as some of our own seem to reject everything we stand for. We get word that a family is headed for divorce, and we just want to go into a cave. In Mark 4, Jesus tells the story of the sower. The sower could not know in advance where to find the best soil, so he broadcast the seed in all directions.

As a pastor, you may extend a helping hand to a family, share your testimony, preach your heart out, launch discipleship and evangelism classes, find ways to serve your community, host a weekly devotion or Bible study, and boldly pray for others. The story seems to indicate that the sower was responsible for making the effort even though only one in four seeds matured. When it comes to eternal matters, you will never be held accountable for the responses of others. But you are accountable for making the efforts. Sometimes success simply means sowing.

# RESPONDING TO MOCKERS

*Whoever corrects a mocker invites insult; whoever rebukes a wicked man incurs abuse. Do not rebuke a mocker or he will hate you; rebuke a wise man and he will love you. Instruct a wise man and he will be wiser still; teach a righteous man and he will add to his learning.*

**Proverbs 9:7-9**

In Proverbs, "mockers" are characterized by an unwillingness to address character issues. Inevitably, this unwillingness leads to destructive behaviors. The question for pastors becomes–"What do we expect of these mockers?" Apart from a relational encounter with Jesus Christ, mockers will consistently act in line with their character–or lack thereof. Proverbs says that to expect otherwise is simply foolishness.

On the other hand, when we correct or challenge someone we have been entrusted to lead, and they respond with gratitude and show us a genuine effort to address personal character issues, we should pour ourselves into them.

Far too many pastors invest far too much time in chasing mockers for all the wrong reasons. Pastors who compromise their integrity by engaging ungrateful mockers, hoping for some earthly reward or recognition while neglecting the long-term opportunities with others who are eager to grow, find themselves insulted, used-up, and worn-out.

# YOUR GAME PLAN

*Therefore go and make disciples of all nations, baptizing them in the name of the Father and of the Son and of the Holy Spirit, and teaching them to obey everything I have commanded you. And surely I am with you always, to the very end of the age.*

**Matthew 28:19-20**

Jesus had a clear understanding about what mattered most, what he expected of his team, what they would need, and how they were doing. He also clearly communicated and reinforced each expectation.

Great leaders understand the need to know and communicate what matters most, what they expect of their team, what they will need, and how they are doing. Paul "Bear" Bryant, the legendary Alabama football coach, had five points that explained what he believed a coach should do:

- Tell players what you expect of them.
- Give players an opportunity to perform.
- Let players know how they are getting along.
- Instruct and empower players when they need it.
- Reward players according to their contributions.

What's your game plan? What matters most? What do you expect of each team member? What will they need? How are they doing? Have you communicated each of these to each of them?

# NOTHING IS IMPOSSIBLE

*I can do all things through him who strengthens me.*

**Philippians 4:13**

Nothing is impossible for the God who spoke the world into existence. Which of your concerns might overwhelm the God who parted the Red Sea, healed the sick, gave sight to the blind, raised the dead, cast out demons, could not be tempted, and overcame death?

Comparing his strength to ours is like comparing a locomotive to a microbe; His power, like comparing a nuclear reactor to a firefly.

And Paul says his power strengthens us. Who could stand against us? When we stop treating him like a flash light, a genie in a bottle, or a pharmacist filling our prescription, and trust him to provide exactly what we need, nothing is impossible. Just read the stories of Moses, Noah, Elijah, David, Joseph, and Peter.

# LIGHT

*Iamthelightoftheworld.Whoeverfollowsmewillnever walk in darkness, but will have the light of life.*

**John 8:12**

I found the following definitions regarding properties of objects interacting with light on my daughter's science homework:

Opaque—No visible light passes through. No image can be seen.

Translucent—Some light passes through, but the material distorts the image.

Transparent—Most light passes through, allowing a clear image to be seen.

My mind immediately went to my willingness to allow Christ to be seen through me in my everyday interactions. When you consider Jesus as the light of the world, which of the three properties best describes you today? What if we asked your members? Your co-workers? Your family? Your friends?

# THE LION'S ROAR

*A king's rage is like the roar of a lion, but his favor is like dew on the grass.*

**Proverbs 19:12**

Some pastors seem to think it's all about them. Everything revolves around their own plans, goals, and desires. Their idea of a team is a collection of people doing whatever they tell them to do. Just step back, listening to them rant and rave, and you might just see some similarities between them and a naturally self-centered two-year-old.

The lion's roar is one of the most fearsome sounds in all of nature. But, as awesome as a lion's roar is, it would become commonplace, losing its impact, if it was heard throughout each day. A wise leader knows that consistent encouragement is needed to temper and balance his roar in order to cultivate unity, trust, stability, passion, hope, competence, clarity, and discipline.

For more information about
# JOHN CROSBY
## &
### CALLED TO SHEPHERD
please visit:

*www.priorityinsight.com*
*john@priorityinsight.com*
*www.facebook.com/PriorityInsight*

. . . . . . . . . . . . . . . . . . . . . . . . . . . . . . . . . . . . . . . . . . . . . . . . . . .

For more information about
## AMBASSADOR INTERNATIONAL
please visit:

*www.ambassador-international.com*
*@AmbassadorIntl*
*www.facebook.com/AmbassadorIntl*

Made in the USA
Middletown, DE
04 August 2021